D0867759

THE SILENT TREATMENT

The Silent Treatment

∞

NEW POEMS

Richard Howard

TURTLE POINT PRESS
NEW YORK

Some of these poems originally appeared elsewhere:

"In Loco Parentis," *Georgia Review*; "The Silent Treatment," *Salmagundi*;
"An After-Dinner Speech," *Boulevard*; "Attachments," *Boston Review*; "Sitting
to Paul," *Colorado Review*; "From the Minutes," *Cincinnati Review*; "To a Friend
Completing Her Biography of Hawthorne," *New Yorker*; "A Mistaken Identity,"
Michigan Quarterly Review; "Arendt: An Arguable Elegy," *Yale Review*; "George and
Ethel Gage with Mother Ida Gage and Their First Five Children," *Daedalus*;
"A Thief in the Night, or *Lettres Philosophiques*," *Western Humanities Review*;
"A Faun's Afternoon," *Yale Review*

ISBN 1-885586-38-8
Library of Congress Catalogue Number 2004113837

COVER IMAGE: *Nine Caves and Their Inhabitants*
Natalie Charkow Hollander
courtesy of Lohin Geduld Gallery, NYC

Printed in Canada

Donald Justice
d. 2004

Anthony Hecht
d. 2004

Mona Van Duyn
d. 2004

. . . to earth o'er given,
these the companions
—EZRA POUND

CONTENTS

THE SILENT TREATMENT

In Loco Parentis

Not now, Charles. Just leave the wine,
we'll help ourselves . . . (Always fussing, except
   when you need them.) I do want
our lunch to be *festive*, Naomi. You know
   how I've gloried, this past year,

in all your achievements . . . You're really
   our star editor now—a feat
for a *fête*. But before the *soufflé* arrives
   (I know how you love dessert)
give me a moment: I want to discuss

   something intimate. Not just
about you or me, but *us*: that's what makes it
   intimate. I think you know
how this has happened, hour by hour, day after
   day, as you sat at your desk

                    *   *   *

in the office next to mine, learning more
  than anything I could teach—
I would step in and watch you getting through
  a dish of *crème brûlée* as if
it were a lost chapter of Flaubert,

  and then restoring a page
of Kahlil Gibran to the superior
  crème brûlée the author meant
his pie in the sky to become all along;
  the fact is, my dear, you were

teaching *me* what a publisher can do
  and as I learned you became,
in the gradual process, a sort of
  sagacious daughter to me:
the girl I never had with Alfred . . . And in you

  I see—just beginning, dear—
what has turned my flesh to ash, and what I would
  spare you if I could. Once I . . .
I used to be a different woman, Naomi.
  Let me tell you a story . . .

*   *   *

In 1923 Alfred took me to Paris
    and every day, after lunch,
we ritually went to the Louvre. Once,
    coming down the staircase from
the Victory of Samothrace, we passed two

elderly gentlemen climbing up, the one
    near me staring hard. And just
as Alfred mouthed "Blanche, that's Conrad!"
    the man himself murmured
"*Quelle belle Juive!*" Ever since that day,

    I've stopped eating (eating as
I like to eat) and never started again.
    It's gone on for forty years,
my resolve not to become what I had been:
    a *zaftig* Yiddle, the kind

"admired," so to speak, by dirty old men.
    When (rarely) I'm tempted to
éclairs or *crèpes Suzette*, I can see her,
    that slim, flat-bellied Greek girl
at the top of the stairs, and I still hear

the Pole's hateful appraisal . . .
Naomi, I'm won't prescribe breast reduction,
   I'm not your mother, am I?
But take for yourself the omen, the sign
   given me back then, and gain

where I lost, or lose where I had gained:
   at your age, it will be simple
and quick too; you won't suffer long, merely
   qualify your hungers. Shall we
begin today? Charles, cancel the *soufflé*.

The Silent Treatment

for Natalie Charkow Hollander, sculptor

After La Spezia our train shadowed
    the Ligurian coast through
  a blind repetition of tunnels
  on its promised route to Genoa,
    though not at all promising
were those deafening darknesses, sudden

stretches of inhumation during which
    my own face at the window
  (now but a bituminous mirror)
  became a sort of luminous ghost
    instantaneously
exorcised by an unforeseeable

glimpse of glistening sea enclosed by crags
    and, right under that window,
  what appeared to be naked
  cadavers—but then vision vanished,
    the tunnels resumed, and we
were in the dark, maybe this time for good!

*　*　*

Good or bad, such glimpses (and framing glooms)
　　　have afforded me a clue,
　　dear devious artist, to what you
　　　have created, casting the first stones,
　　　　so to speak, which you then carve
and call, in that conversant way of yours,

Reliefs, indeed *Reliefs in Stone*—as if
　　　　assuagement were to be had
　　　from that quarter, that . . . quarry. There is
　　cold comfort in a slab of limestone
　　　　shielding from us a slice of . . .
life? What are they up to, those mute figures

never delivered from the living rock
　　　　yet laboring for dear life
　　against it? No time to find out. Like
　　my train in its unguessed tunnels,
　　　　revealing and revoking
sunlight, sea, and those prostrate beached bodies,

* * *

your "Mythological Views" dispel their
    apparitions once they have
  appeared. The intervals correspond
  to those unlooked-for tunnel visions:
    the same yet altogether
otherwise, a rhythm consonant with

the heart's desire and yet obedient
    to the decrees of fate. So
  only after that providential
  train ride could I have seen through
    your tactic to derail us
by invoking the hallowed precedent

of classical (i.e., unoffending)
    Masters of the Mythical:
  ("Scenes from Ovid," "After Poussin," or
  "Regarding Piero"). But this once
    such stratagems fail you, and
as if forced to disclose your true intent,

you give to one harrowing—and harrowed—
   white marble impertinence
   —dated '97 and bound with
   a strip of funerary black slate
   for defiant emphasis—
the name "Nine Caves & Their Inhabitants,"

as if to defy what could be made out
   of creatures and occasions
   not consenting to be seen: "inmates"
   (surely the right word) on the other
   side—for us, the wrong side—
of that perforated snowy shroud. Art,

according to Charkow's will (and to half
   the world before history—
   item: Ajanta, Luxor, Lascaux),
   art was not necessarily meant
   to be seen, not intended
for human eyes, in fact. And you, my dear,

have joined the self-immolating moilers
     of Easter Island or
   Chichén Itzá, for in your reliefs
   Life and Light are secrets carried on
     without the accessory
of merely human onlookers. Life here,

—heroic or mere, festive or routine—
     simmers always just beyond
   a riddled gray sandstone barrier;
   everyone's backs are always to us—
     another parable of caves,
or, as you put it, "Four Places to Hide."

And as for Light, only so much leaks in
     as might limn the mystery
   of form. Stone, thus edified, offers
   little to distinguish *him* from *her*,
     fighting from fucking, as Freud
learned from peeking children. (Details, details.)

*　　*　　*

The great thing—no, the whole thing—well, the real
　　thing is what goes on inside
　the stone or else on the other side
　as you secretively let us have it,
　　poor onlookers poorly fed
by the rations of art which has its own

conplicity with life, and not with us.
　　Art's relentless triangle
　—the makers, their lives, their leavings (say,
　twelve stone reliefs)—more often than not
　　leave us out (do you care?
can you even tell?) of its eternal

geometry. I learned this on a train
　　up the coast of Italy,
　seizing those sudden shards of light
　—of *life*—from intermittent darkness,
　　and then here to face again
these hiding places of yours in the stone

which even when it's gray—or when it's white!—
    is dark. Stone is our dark lot,
   and only a hidden life is there
    to be looked for, not found. Give me your caves,
     show me what there is to see:
"Reliefs in stone," my dear, for which these thanks.

An After-Dinner Speech

loquitur : *Anton Raphael Mengs,*
Court Painter–elect to Charles III of Spain

*S*ignori, you have my gratitude for
the *signal* honor
of this banquet, the learned discourses,
                 as well as, of course,
the great distinction of your company.
"Old Mengs," you call me
among yourselves, and it is true: I am
                 old now—old at least
in our shared habituation, so that
for me to forsake
our Rome is a hazardous enterprise.
                 For many years now
I have expended what powers I have
as the director
of this Academy—this fellowship,
                 I had rather say—
which a number of us assembled here
founded together;

and were it not for His Majesty's
                    summons to Madrid
—an appeal scarcely to be resisted—
you should not find me
leaving you today (or next October,
                    to be more precise) . . .

Looking back—the customary action
performed, I believe,
on such occasions, in order to move
                    forward, or at least
in some sense outward—I find that I have
two declarations
worthy, I must believe, of your notice.
                    First, it was my fate,
my fortune, indeed my felicity,
to translate the laws
formulated first by the immortal
                    Winckelmann—the laws
of Grecian beauty into plastic terms.
How often we heard
his stern admonishment: without the Greeks
                    no salvation, no

hope for those who refuse to discipline
their genius! Born
in Greece, guarded by Imperial Rome
                    ere being engulfed
by Gothic ignorance, this Ideal Art
was given into
our keeping by my guide, my compatriot,
                    and my dearest friend
who honored me by the dedication
of his glorious
History of Ancient Art among the Greeks,
                    and it is his rule
alone that I have striven to uphold—
I have made it mine,
and it must be the heritage I leave
                    to those who follow . . .

Such fealty is the first and likeliest
asseveration
I can offer in response to your own.
                    Perhaps the second
will disconcert you, yet it constitutes

a spirited proof
of the very ideals we celebrate
                    tonight . . . You may recall
when young Benjamin West arrived in Rome,
none of us conceived
he would succeed Reynolds as President,
                    eventually,
of the Royal Academy. Not that
he offered no signs
of talent, but after all, being born
                    in the wild country
around Philadelphia . . . Here in the very
City of the Popes,
some believed the boy might well be a Red
                    Indian himself!
It was worth testing Winckelmann's premise
that the Apollo
Belvedere (which we more properly call
                    Apollo Venator)
is the first statue in the world. So we stood
young Ben West (young then
as I am old Mengs now) in the courtyard

of the Belvedere
and threw open the great doors of the niche
in which the god stood
(in the most agreeable attitude
                    that could be confined
in a niche), in order to discover
the impression made
by perfection on the untutored mind.
                    Whereupon it came:
"My God!" exclaimed the youth, "how like it is
to a Mohawk brave!"
Apollo the Hunter, indeed. *Signori*,
                    Was that not simple?
Was that not splendid? Was that not even
surpassing Greek?
There is the Ideal for you. For me. I rest
                    my case, and bid you,
gratefully, a good night. I know I shall
lack Rome in Madrid,
but I cherish such memories as these—
                    they will make up for
much that is missing. *Signori*, adieu!

Attachments

to the Apollo Belvedere

i   Goethe

Of course I was pleased
        to find the figure
                has great intrinsic
                merit, aside from
            its celebrity,
    to recommend it.

ii   Preferring to it The Hermaphrodite
                    which is in an adjoining niche,
        Her Highness called the statue "the only
                    happy couple she ever saw."

iii   No less an arbiter than Canova
        has indicated the seven points
            from which the radiant god
                may be readily studied
                to best advantage;

*   *   *

    (for a trifling sum
     a copy of this precious
   diagram may be purchased
  from any of the attendants
    in the Belvedere courtyard)

iv The evident high breeding of the god
          has always been apparent;
   as Hippolyte Taine himself remarked,
         Apollo must have had servants.

v Classical Simplicity demands a Static Port.
       Indeed Count d'Orsay,
  who believed it impossible to approve statues in action
 for longer than he himself could stand in the same attitude,
       was once heard to say
 he felt able to admire the Apollo for hours . . . even for days!

To which with some spirit Lady Blessington offered
     her famous *réplique*:
"The god with his arm outstretched and a heavy blanket on it

wearies *me* after five minutes! Of course my fatigue might be
relieved, dear Alfred,
were it you in that very costume who had taken that very pose."

vi The Novelist and the Naturalist

"Once he was holding something, George. Just look!
his fingers are still
curled round an invisible spear—perhaps
to kill a dragon . . ."

"Far from trying to kill the serpent, Marian,
it is more likely
the god was merely stimulating it with a dart
so as to rouse it
from its hibernation. Dragons are boreal . . ."

vii Suggesting that the god had been removed
from Greece by Nero,
Herr Winckelmann was never quite happy
with the piece, and his
unqualified enthusiasm was limited
to the legs and knees.

*   *   *

viii   Monsieur Beyle studied it
                     like something from China,
              but it aroused, he said,
                     neither pain nor pleasure.

From the Diary of Cosima Wagner

*As if any record of the entire episode were distasteful to her,
the diarist appears to have torn material concerning three days
—May 15, 16, and 17, 1877—out of the buckram binding
of the volume for that year. Survival and recovery of these
pages have never been adequately explained.*

London. Monday. Rain and fog give a ghostly
   look to the city—it is just here,
in this swarming hive of human exertion,
   that I have been made most mindful of
the phantasmagoria, the *oneiric*
   nature of Life. One begins to doubt
even the buildings: they are there, then vanish . . .
   How unlike Italian palaces!
R declares this is Alberich's dream come true
   —Nibelheim, the world of Dominion—
yet birds sing, even in fog, and we have heard
   nightingales during a thunderstorm:
R says they must take the thunder for applause.
   A great city, yes, but crowded with

*   *   *

meager citizens—so mundane, so greedy
    I marvel how they manage to give
the illusion of munificence. *Who pays?*
    as Englishmen say, or better still
Who is paid to provide? I know for a fact
    that R has received, for conducting
eight concerts, paltry sums, most of which he gives
    to the poor musicians, still worse off
than he. There can be no hope of covering
    costs: the public has already been
bullied by the Press and by Herr Joachim
    (Brahms's friend and, of course, a Jew),
nor am I at all certain that we shall be
    able to return First Class to Wahnfried.

The whole of Israel is once more working
    against us. As R says: *What are we*
Germans? Who can say? All we know is that
    we are stripped bare by the Jews and clothed
by the French. First thing, R's tormenting molar
    was attended to ("fixed") by a Jew
dentist (Marx!) who refused to accept payment

(but then he is an American).
In yesterday's *Zeitung* R has discovered
    the death of his first Isolde, poor
Ernestine Schroeder-Devrient, and doubtless
    inspired by his molar ordeal, made
the apposite, cruel, and inevitable
    witticism: *I have lost a false tooth.*

"Isolde" reminds me: English management
    now insists that R eliminate
T & I from the programs. R disgusted,
    but impassive too: is it *his* loss?
Our first day in this city inhabited
    chiefly by downpours (and dreams, of course):
how we walked!—past the Tower, the Abbey, then
    some way along the Thames to the hall
where a small crowd had collected to catch sight
    of R arriving for rehearsal—
the square I find much disfigured by a new
    synagogue—insolent, sumptuous!
To think there were no Jews here for centuries!
—Yet how kind the English are, kindest

*   *   *

of all, Papa's friend the critic George Lewes
    who had visited him in Weimar
years ago (the authoress of *Adam Bede*
    being *attached* to him then, just as
the Princess Sayn-Wittgenstein was to Papa!
    O the bravery of such women!),
whereupon Papa prevailed on "George Eliot"
    to translate his new essay: "Wagner
and Meyerbeer"—impossible companions!—
    which Mr Lewes then published here
in England! Now he insists I call him *George*
    and I must strive to be familiar,
though I don't like to, when *she* sets so much store
    by being addressed as *"Mrs* L."

George then (oh dear, not *that* George) appears so
    genuinely eager that we meet
some true spirits of Culture—and who could find
    fault with *him* if such encounters
must inevitably disappoint? (R is
    forever rehearsing, but I know
his response would be my own . . .) Why, only

today I was taken (by George) to
the Grosvenor Gallery, a shrine of "taste"
    which, together with a complete
disregard for economy, rules the gaudy
    premises. Here I was shown
a painting (at least the daub was in a *frame*)
    entitled for all to see (and hear?)

"Nocturne in Black & Gold: The Falling Rocket"
    which the press, for lack of classical
form and clear subject, had called "Wagnerian."
    This I was told with a detestable smirk
by the artist himself (Siffleur or Sisley?)
    I never caught the name)—and was I
to commiserate with him for the affront?
    Oh no, George (subsequently) explained:
this little creature with the one white lock (dyed?)
    in his untidy mop of gray curls
and sporting both a monocle *and* a cane
    merely meant to cite the papers' use
of the "invidious adjective" as tribute
    to his own art as it was to R's.

* * *

Wagnerian . . . Could this absurd creature share
    any adjective, or verb, or noun
with R? Mime perhaps, one tag that might be
    aptly applied as "Wagnerian"!
Tuesday's "true spirit," my cicerone swore,
    would prove more rewarding; this would be
William Morris, big and blunt as the painter
    of rockets had been barbed and bantam.
And I was warned that Morris might allude to
    still another *Nibelungenlied*,
his own saga of *Sigurd the Volsung*, and
    indeed, as we entered the print shop,
behold the poet himself, both hands as blue
    as printer's ink could make them. "You must

forgive me, *my nature is subdued to what*
    it works in, like the dyer's hand. Quite
literally, my dear lady. How d'you do?"
    His features had assumed the aspect
of quotation, and so of course *I* assumed
    —correctly, as it happened—the words
were Shakespeare's, citing whom (in England) bids fair

to exonerate whatever's said
thereafter. Even so, I was ill-prepared
  for the outburst of mannerlessness:
"I haven't heard much of your husband's music,
  can't make out his poetry at all—
rather a panto version of the affair,
    don't y'know—I suppose I must wait

till the Transformation Scene to judge at all
    fairly: even pantomime may have
its thrilling moments." *To judge at all fairly* . . .
  And this boor's company must be borne
tomorrow night, when the two Georges have asked
    R to read (to a German-speaking conclave
quite unaware it is to hear the poem,
    only just finished, of *Parsifal*—
a privilege as yet enjoyed by no one
    in Bayreuth!), and Morris will be *there*.
How I writhe at the very notion of this
  entertainer ready and waiting
"to judge at all fairly" our sacred dream-play,
    the crown of Richard Wagner's life . . .

                    *   *   *

Wednesday is past: a triumph, of course, for R.
    Morris himself was overheard to concede
R spoke with great spirit and skill. I myself
    observed how his *presence*, as always,
dwarfed that of all others in the room. There were,
    to be sure, various "trouble spots."
I have come to expect and almost to relish
    these things in England, especially
in the company of "spirits of Culture,"
    as Lewes so pathetically
accounted them to me. But I was deeply
    pained as well as taken by surprise
that one of these incidents was occasioned
    by "Mrs Lewes" who had, these weeks,

become almost a friend, or so I had thought.
    Right off, it had been a great relief
from my wretched boarding-school English that she
    (and he as well!) spoke fluent German.
And in a woman of true accomplishments
    (I read *Marner* and *The Mill* with much
enjoyment) to find such unassuming airs!

Never, despite those terrible last
sentences of hers, shall I cease to cherish
    the earlier ones, which might almost
be regarded—though doubtless not by herself—
    as an acknowledgment of weakness,
or at least an inaptitude shared by a large part
    of a less-gifted humanity.

How seldom we observe more than one aspect
    of our friends, as we see but one side
of the moon. There is a dark side too, unknown
    to us. We all come down to dinner,
but upstairs each has a chamber to herself . . .
    I suppose I might have realized
more than I had allowed myself to divine
    about this deceptive woman's soul
had I troubled to read her latest novel,
    published just before our arrival
and concerned, I hear, with Jews exclusively.
    A mere glance at the dedication
—*To my dear husband George Henry Lewes*—
reveals her ruthless duplicity,

                    *   *   *

and then I might have been less practiced upon
    by her subsequent wiles (she is not
a fabulist for nothing, though this *Deronda*
    of hers is said to be nothing but
philo-Semitic *rant*). I should have guessed . . .
    After attending two rehearsals
and the final performance where she caught cold
    (she is terribly susceptible
for a large woman) she wrote me this: *We are*
    but in the first morning of the times
and must learn to consider ourselves as mere
    tadpoles unprescient of the future
frog. And still the tadpole is limited to
    tadpole joys. So, in our present state

of advancement, we are swayed by melody.
    Sixteen years back, at my initial
Lohengrin, *I missed the melody my ear*
    requires. Sixteen years on, we are still
arrested in the tadpole stage. And just three days
    after sending these apparently
candid phrases, this same learned (however

unmusical) lady at her own

house party, given in my husband's honor,

    came up to me, drew me aside, and

with that straightforwardness so conspicuous

    in her character, uttered these words:

I hear you and your husband too hate the Jews.

    You must know my husband is a Jew.

I know he is not. That "noble" false avowal

    was a mere provocation designed

to wound a new friend and indeed to destroy

    that double friendship which so seldom

grows between two couples. If George Lewes sees

    a Jew in every bush, then let him

cultivate shrubbery . . . He is not a Jew,

    nor will he rally us to their cause

by lying that he is. I hate her for it,

    hate him for allowing her to use

him if he knows, and if he does *not* know,

    I hate them both the more. Another

case of *Perfidious Albion*, of which

    I shall tell R . . . nothing whatever.

Sitting to Paul

A meditation on a memory
for Lizette Georges

No wonder the French use the word *séance*
        for the sessions painters need
in order to *get through* to their portrait
            —of course it's theirs, the *painters'*
portrait, being merely *of* the sitter,
        who's no more than a pretext—

a *séance* is exactly what it is,
        for as I was to find out,
the sitting—or their multiplication:
        how many? I lost count—was
indeed a *séance* in the spooky sense,
        a magical summoning

of spirits who appeared, grimaced, and were
        gone, giving way to others
just as irrelevant in the painter's
        view of the matter, and were

therefore scrubbed out, painted over, although
        to me they looked perfectly

fine, finer than myself—"O leave it, Paul!
        that's just how I want to look"
(which apparently had nothing to do
        with the picture Paul Georges
wanted to paint). It grew quite bothersome
        to see myself be undone

so many times, just when I imagined
        I had come to speaking terms
with myself (at least in Paul's eyes and
        in Paul's hands—which had to be
the whole point, no?). For this ceremony
        of disillusion resumed

day after unsubstantiated day,
        week after nullifying week:
the portrait was never finished although
        the *séances* came to an end.
"You can have the thing, if that's what you want.
        It's not mine, in any case—

* * *

no painting of mine." Rest assured, I own
        another Georges or two,
in particular, a woman walking
        into the sea—I know your
thighs, Lizette, and those have got to be
        the waves at Georgica Beach!

But what would never be Richard finished
        is in a closet, waiting . . .
As you waited too, Paul, as we all wait
        for the hands to complete us
which made so many faces, so much life,
        still life and stirring, then stopped.

From the Minutes

of the Acquisitions Committee
of the Bodleian Library, Oxford University
Professor Alfred Hemming in the Chair

The document before you,
on offer (at a preposterous asking price)
and of a mysterious provenance, offers
indeed a great mystery or perhaps
      merely mystification
with regard to the Conrad Dossier. And with
regard to Conrad himself, as has been said,
mystery and mystification come
      down to the same thing. So much
for literary criticism, gentlemen.
Furthermore, it is your Chair's opinion
that the 'Rimbaud hypothesis' advanced
      by this singular vendor
and already familiar to this Committee
is yet again a hoax—'*Doctor Will Resink*'
sounds altogether bogus to me, even if

he is, as he claims, a Serb.
Especially in view of the maritime
or perhaps I should say *marine* nature
of the circumstances, concerning which
        Professor Resink (really!)
provides what any less covetous scholar
than this Balkan pretender, as I make him out,
would regard as suspect proliferation
        of superficial details—
just look at his prefatory pronouncements,
all that flashy citing of possible dates
and parallel schedules: ". . . the one week in which
        they *could* meet, because Rimbaud,
who had suffered sunstroke in Leghorn, returned
to France instead of going on to Algiers,
disembarking at Marseilles on June 18,
        perhaps into hospital,
and we know for a fact that on June 25
young Jozef Korzeniowski (on his first
trans-oceanic voyage, having signed on
        as an apprentice), sailed for
Martinique on the brig *Mont Blanc . . .*" Whereupon

our shameless huckster proceeds to declare
the crude scholiae before you constitute
           evidence of a meeting,
indeed of an intimacy, which neither
party to it, from what we know of either,
would have countenanced a moment! Gentlemen,
           consider the document!
(One wonders, of course, how such a thing managed
to turn up in Kosovo, of all places?
I daresay we'll soon be hearing of its
           purchase by the Maecenas
of Malibu or some other moneybags
in the States . . . That bugger in Austin will buy
whatever savors of pederasty.) Herewith:

> *He does not love the sea, of course,*
> *only man-against the sea, and never*
> *understood when I talked about*
> > *the sea itself . . .*
>
> *I think he must have disliked what I*
> *showed him, written last year:*
> >   *   *   *

'I am the scholar in a dark armchair.
Branches thrash against the library window,
and I am the child abandoned on a pier
                              washed out to sea.

Then I could hear the waves dragging their
evening gowns into the cove.

For years I had dreamed of uniting with
my double. Remembering, I realized
I had always been someone else.
                              Believing in

nothing that was past, I believed
only in truth established by metaphor.

Now I realize that in the realm of time
I must submit to the domination
of the sole power I had created:
                              transformation.

All that I learned is lies. I gained
nothing by knowing. I gained nothing.

*   *   *

What I have comes to me through
the union of silence and the sea.
                    Perhaps the desert . . .'

We are asked to believe (and
to pay for our credulity!) that these notes,
purported to be in Arthur Rimbaud's hand,
were composed in an English, to call it that,
        which the poet prodigy
(and pervert) had learned in patches as he had
already acquired the chief tongues of Europe
(I leave the choice to your own discretion)
        on his peregrinations, to which
he would add a sort of pidgin Arabic . . .
Though of course he knew our language better than
the adolescent Pole we are to assume
        he is alluding to here.
O shameless imposture, venality, greed!
To be sure, I have combed the correspondence
for clues. Once only does Conrad refer to
        Rimbaud, and not at all as

any sort of acquaintance: "I happen
to know his verses, can't understand Rimbaud
at all." This in '99! to his old friend
        Cunning-Graham, followed by
a joke: "I wish you would come and shoot me."
I perceive from your demeanor, gentlemen,
that a vote is supererogatory. There can be
        no doubt our Resink is a fraud.
My apologies for requiring so much
of your time and your attention, though of course
we are obligated to consider any *likely*
        addition to our holdings:
I am pleased to accept your concurrence that
this proposal is no such thing. Gentlemen,
the case is closed, and our meeting as well. Thank you.

To a Friend Completing
Her Biography of Hawthorne

"We were not, it is true, so well acquainted
       at college that I can plead
a classmate's undisputed right to inflict
       my 'twice-told' tediousness
upon you, yet I have been glad of your own
       success in literature,
and in more important matters."
                              What had been
       —what *could* have been, I wonder—
"more important" to Hawthorne, sequestered for
       a dozen years in Salem,
struggling to make himself a writer? And for
       his initially cautious
correspondent, the fatally fluent
       Henry Wadsworth Longfellow,
savoring the first of those dread successes:
       for him, too, could there have been
matters more important than literature?

                    *   *   *

And then of course I wonder
about you and me—about all of our tribe,
    whom Montaigne identified
without contempt as *la gent écrivassière*,
    secreted so manageably,
as luck would have it, in this apprehensive
    and inadvertent city—
whether it is something of the same kind
    that every dreaming midnight
and every waking dawn glows (*glowers*) for us
    like the radium on our clocks,
matters *more important than literature.*

A Mistaken Identity

to Craig Morgan Teicher, whom I recognized
as the model for Rubens's earliest dated work,
Portrait of a Young Man *(in the Linsky
Gallery of the Metropolitan Museum)*, inscribed
on the back Petrus Paulus Rubens *and on
the front* 1597 *along with the sitter's age,* 26.

What was it *like*? No one I've ever known
comes close to your qualifications for
    telling . . . Who else could resolve
that paradox *the present of the past*
better than someone visibly hand-picked,
    as it were, to be its living
substantiation? It was *quite by chance*
(such episodes generally begin
    with those words, a formula
fabricated to avoid any and
all charges of intention or desire
    for whatever might occur)
that I walked through the Linsky Gallery
(I try to avoid those museum rooms
    gussied up with a lot of

period dreck—astrolabes and theorbos—
the paintings in them are usually
        the kind called "decorative")
and there you were, intimately present
in a position (and in a *posture*)
            to observe everything
in front of you but what was taking shape
in the hands of a grimacing master
        (seven years your junior—
later on, he learned not to make faces
at important clients: royalty seldom
        relishes being scowled at).
And you must have guessed, even if you were
unimportant, that something remarkable
        was coming into being
on the copper sheet which was the one thing
you couldn't see—why else do you suppose
        old Otto van Veen (*Vaenius*
he must be called now that he's been chosen
Dean of the Painters' Guild of Saint Luke)
        kept slipping into the room
to peer over the cold shoulder of this

prodigy who was still his apprentice?
     And I could see for myself,
despite your worldly trappings, that a somewhat
transcendent effect was being sought here—
     who could take a countenance
like yours, every feature commingling in
the gravity of innocence, for a merely
     marketable likeness,
the tyro's flattering competence? In fact
I presume that precisely *because*
     the borrowed workshop behind
the "unknown sitter" was dark, was *Stygian*,
the sudden whiteness of that splendid ruff
     (did you learn how frequently
they have to be changed, and how they're *cleaned*?
such things can't just be thrown away, can they?)
     encircled your head and beard
within a sort of upside-down halo—
the effect *was* a sort of saintliness,
     an abstergent hiatus
separating the face I recognize
from that doublet you had on, black velvet

slashed with white satin ribbons,
its round onyx buttons catching the light
so that they too looked white . . . Well, for all
    the deceptions of darkness,
I could observe the gestures you appeared
to be ignoring even as you made them
    (you were staring at Rubens):
on a ledge, your right hand, skin transparent,
veins prominent (I'd noticed that before),
    was holding a pair of bronze
dividers and a square—architects' tools,
or a cartographer's—did you ever
    discover what they were for?
and that oval doodad suspended by
a red cord from your left thumb? Most likely
    a gold-chased watch—in terms of
art history, a *memento mori*,
affording what might be regarded as
    a deliberate contrast
to your carefully rehearsed and performed
youth. Yet such ostentatious finery,
    effective as it was, failed

to make the man your clothes had made of you
into anyone but my former student,

   my contemporary friend
whose youth I have rehearsed with an equal
solicitude on my own premises . . .

   It was that intricate ear
of yours, Craig, refuting a Flemish neck,
which gave the baroque masquerade away—

   unmistakably naked
and quite distinct from your baroque drag
(like a sort of fresh-water clam fastened

   behind your cheekbone). Rubens
couldn't have studied it more closely than I,
and I'm quite prepared to authenticate

   a Twenty-First-Century ear!
Your hair was "modern" too—a chestnut pelt
which only oil-paint on copper transcribes

   with such organic gusto
(when the transcribing brushwork
comes from the hands of Peter Paul Rubens) . . .

   All the same, I'd say that hair
was more likely "done" by Frederic Fekkai

or possibly Mitzu on Madison—
        who in Antwerp had such hair?
And the left side of your moustache, curling
so carefully, absorbing the light
        as the sparks fly upward? Just
between us, I couldn't help noticing
the fingernails of your left hand (the one
        holding a watch or perhaps
an astrolabe—some mystical and sumptuous
device with which your American hands
        seemed completely unconcerned)
looked just as grimy as they did last year
        in my comp-lit classes when
you ran the slide projector for me.
Are those the nails we want to see sported
        by our man-about-Antwerp?
Somehow, Craig, despite or perhaps because
of your appearance in a past with which
        neither of us dreamed you had
anything to do, I feel we've both failed
to make contact, as mediums always claim
        they can with *the other side*.

It seems to me you're either *here* and *then*
or *there* and *now,* which is no assistance
          either way (though in logic
it should be), and for all my positive
recognition (*identification!*) of
          your flesh-and-blood appearance
in an early Rubens, I'm not getting
the real right stuff from you. I started out
          asking you what it was like,
—by "it" I meant no less than "being alive"
then and there—but I received no response.
          Why can't you be more helpful
about personal hygiene *ab illo tempore*—
say, dirty nails? We know what we think
          of the past, we need to know
what the past thinks of us. It ought to work
like a sort of charm, a formula:
          Take a square inch of Rubens
(say a patch from the palm of your left hand),
          magnify it to the size
of a Rothko and you get . . . a Rothko. But
a square inch of Rothko magnified (or

even reduced) will not come
close to a Rubens—only a Rothko!
I'm trying to tell you we go forward
        but not back, where the past is,
and the past makes no effort to reach us.
Between a Tudor portrait and a Twombly
        no correspondences, no
transfers—no round trip at all! It's the same
paralysis in all the arts. Listen,
        in spite of the learned praise
a composer like Boulez showers on
Clément Jannequin, no likely echo
        will be received so long as
we lack any clue to what that old French
madrigalist makes of, say, *Pli selon Pli*.

        Yet there you were with Rubens,
so possibly Rubens was there with you . . .
Craig, I counted on you for some sort
        of mutual evidence
that it's all one enterprise, one . . . nature.
How silly that was, to count on the past—
        even on you in the past.

Nothing's *inevitable* (who could guess
I'd find you in the Linsky Collection?),
          but nothing's *reversible.*
What's the use finding my friend in a fond
likeness if he can't tell me more about
          Rubens and *his* friends (and foes)
than I've already guessed or at least assumed?
Mistaken identities are merely
          magical accidents, not
a form of communion with the Great Dead.
It's become clear to me that time, even
          in the hands of young Rubens—
time can do everything but tell, Craig . . .
Happily there is another means of
          intercourse, outside of time.
It's called the present. It does not exist
until we live in it, unless we live . . .
          I won't look for you again
in the gallery where I know you hang
out. I have a better method. Call me
          now. We'll talk to each other.

Arendt:
An Arguable Elegy

The meaning of memory: effacement
of matter by form. Only
now can I construct likely atmospheres—
now that I have disordered
all the facts—germane to the occasion.
Thirty years after your death
the dates blur, what is remembered becomes
mythology, mine to make . . .

*

i) 1955

Curtained off, the lamplight concentrated
on you—concentrated *you*,
enfolded in the appropriate fumes
from a fane of nicotine,
into an affable growling augur

whose voice (to my tense tenor)
constituted a figured bass on which
    to develop progressions.

Yet only your eyes moved, following smoke
    into darkness, composing
a study less domestic than occult,
    indistinct yet momentous,
until the room was like Rembrandt's portraits:
    golden in the center and
either very deep or strangely empty
    in corners of the canvas.

Each cigarette conspired, and the plot dimmed
    to a consent of silence;
you smoked on, mildly curious if more,
    in certain verses, was meant
than met the ear. The evidently vain
    pleasures of literature
were not, between us, much help. I wondered
    why you had invited me . . .

                    *   *   *

The silence was not golden, just yellow
    under that lamp. "Your poems—
they take such pleasure, but they give none back."
    "They take pains," was my defense.
"I look forward to a time (it will come,
    I'm sure it will) when you can
afford to enjoy more than yourself. Real
    pleasure enjoys not itself

but something else. Pain enjoys itself." More
    smoke, and the face behind it
a parody of pain to mock my own.
    Yes, Rembrandt strikes the right note:
even all that smoke could not obscure you,
    ever darkening counsel . . .
A speaking likeness is the painters' myth,
    the organ of sentiment

an impenetrable mask. My version
    makes your commentary sound
more alien than it may have been. I had shared
    no sentiment of yours, no

season—nothing, say, of what might have been
    spring. Besides, it was autumn,
I guessed, autumn that was your incitement,
    and more formative than spring.

My time was up—you had stipulated
    a look at poems, longer
(however zealous any admirer)
    would be intrusive; I had
my leave to go: uncomfortable though
    kind and altogether sane.
Only madness can afford comfort. Oh,
    how the real world disappoints!

ii) 1971

As heroes in epic poems divined
    the presence of deity:
not directly, of course, but in dreams;
    in certain situations
where obedience seemed luminous;

or when words of mere mortals
—uttered by a nurse, a boy, a dog!—
    intimated the goddess:

that sort of recognition. You crossed
        the State Theater lobby,
Auden ambling beside you, wherefore
        it was no surprise the crowd
parted for the Discourse of the Great;
        but then your eyes—grey
or gray as Athena's—discovered
        me, and a grand smile summoned

your reluctant votary: "Wystan,
        have you met this poet friend
of mine?" He had. The poet friend
        stammered Balanchine's praises,
and the shaming ordeal was over.
        Years later you confided
(I was now just a friend, no longer
        requiring introductions

                *   *   *

advantageous to a "poet friend")
    that later, after *Agon*,
Auden had proposed to you: "He wanted,
    you know, somebody to take
his clothes to the dry cleaners." "*Needed*
    somebody, for sure." "Hardly
a firm foundation for a marriage"—
    which grounds you must have tested

for thirty years with Heinrich Blücher,
    and were they not firm beyond
domestic tasks? "If it were not for
    the possibility of truth,"
you had mused in your *Thought Diaries*,
    "then fidelity would be
synonymous with obstinacy."
    All honor to the goddess.

iii) 1972

Was it the consequence—I fear it was—
of what a feminist would call

my "elementary" feminism of those days
    that when you asked me to arrange ("no fuss")
        a meeting—an evening, in fact—
with Nathalie Sarraute (my old and ancient friend,
    in town for lectures), I seized upon
      your surprising request to ask
to dinner all the women writers whom I knew
    (all eight), not realizing this would be
        exactly what you meant by fuss!
Item: Parallel lionesses never meet.

    That dinner, at least for *the chef* (to grant
        myself the one honorific
I may have deserved) if not for the eight diners,
    was *fraught*: exchanges among these persons
        (variously testing untried
surfaces to see what pressure could be withstood)
    demonstrated that to enjoy something
        and at the same time despise it
is a literary faculty as well as
    a Jewish talent—all of us were Jews
        except the author of *Tropismes*
whom you managed, nonetheless, to *have to yourself*

(who else's French was that suasive?), till you
    and Sarraute swapped cards: a signal
for departure—would I show you to a likely
    taxi corner in the wilds of West Street?
        (Nathalie meanwhile seemed content
to exchange *adversaria* in their own language
    with the seven big cats still in the cage.)
        On the way to Abingdon Square,
I thought to please you by mentioning my attendance
    at "your" Heinrich Blücher's New School lectures—
        for several terms. Apparently
the wrong ones. As I handed you into the cab

    gauchely gushing about his insight, his wisdom
        (surely you agreed: you were *there*
in the last row every Thursday, running the tape recorder;
    you would even absently nod to me.
        Our first encounter had not yet
occurred, and what you were nodding at was the mere
    rightness of my—of *anyone's*—being there),
        I raved on: how "the professor"
managed to meet each student's eyes, binding the class

into what he called an appropriate
pedagogic stance, "*erotic
attention*"—and then, just as I was opening

the cab door, you turned and gently rested
your gloved hand on my shoulder,
and in that low, breathy voice I craved and cringed from
whenever you addressed me, you implored:
"Please, Richard, never speak of it—
don't speak of it again." The taxi pulled into
the dark, and in a darkness of my own
I returned to my dinner guests . . .
This was no final instance, there were many more
engagements, but that unaccountable
interdict remains your last word
in my mind. The spirit that denies—denies what?

Heinrich two years dead, and not to speak
of gratitude for his *sagesse*?
A nerve that I had touched, a misery wakened?
What you don't know always hurts . . . someone else,
that old, unavailing prudence.

Five years later, at your memorial service,
    Mary McCarthy described your last years
        of joyful discovery: "O
the beautiful, beautiful world"—it was New England—
    and how you wished Heinrich had been with you
        "to hear the frogs croaking in tune."
You lie beside him in the Annandale graveyard.

                              *

There are your books, of course, even the books
    of your letters—look there for
answers. But truth is indivisible and
    cannot recognize itself.
What we know of others is the divided
    memory of our moments
with them. Anyone who would acknowledge
    truth must become a liar.

George and Ethel Gage with Mother Ida Gage and Their First Five Children: Loretta, Ida, Baby Ivory, Jesse, & Leon

*photograph from a glass-plate
negative by Mike Disfarmer,* 1939

for Dorothy Gallagher

*R*ubrum, *calla, tiger, day*—
in the beauty of the lilies I was born
in Arkansas, fifth
of a perished tribe. Others have yet
to arrive, but here and now
I am in the middle, Baby Ivory
speaking, though you might
wonder about words from an infant
evidently sound asleep
if not actually dead. And you'd be right:
the stillness held by
all the other people in the pose
is just the mortal humdrum

of a hot August morning in Heber Springs,
                but that baby looks
        out of nature for good—could this be
            one of those Mourning Pictures,
everyone gussied up for the tiny corpse
                to remember them
        in heaven in their Sunday best? No,
            just a family portrait—
Baptists don't bury their babies barefoot. But
        how such a *lump*, even if alive
            on Grandmother Ida's lap,
could be answerable for such palaver . . .
                I suggest two ways
        of dealing with the predicament:
            either grant my disclosures
the confidence you would lavish upon some
                fervent Old Master's
        assorted saints and martyrs having
            a Sacred Conversation
(which is to say, minister yet again to
                the madness of art);
        or else, like any good Baptist here

in Heber Springs (there are no
bad Baptists; and besides, in this town of some
thirty-eight hundred
saved souls who every Sunday
rejoice to attend nineteen
Baptist churches, there are *only* Baptists),
you might attribute
the freakishness of my expressive
behavior to the famous
and in fact infallibly invoked notion
that truth will be found
to proceed in all simplicity
and even complexity
"out of the mouths of babes." Therefore listen up,
even if you think
I'm just repeating meaningless sounds
—*rubrum, calla, tiger, day*—
after Mother Ida, who gave me these words
as my own mantra
(whatever the hell a mantra is—
my infantile omniscience
may be capable of anything, but not

of *everything*),
or maybe just a lullaby, though
to look at Mother Eve—oops!
Mother *Ida*. Sorry, I keep doing that.
It's what Miss Bishop,
with neither a child nor a mother
she ever knew, liked to call
"looking our infant sight away"; which for me
means substituting
a grim crone in a black straw halo
for Piero's sacred hag
who alone among her uncomprehending
brood there in Arezzo
surveys the certainty of Adam's
death and her own. Now Ida,
like ancient Eve, might strike you as unlikely
to sing anything
so comforting as a lullaby.
Look again: can you make out
the way she nestles my minuscule right thumb
in her gnarled left hand?
I'd say there's some sort of cradle-song

in the old ghoul yet. She may
have time on her hands (it won't wash off),
            but love abides too,
    though seeming nothing more than solace . . .
        Over on my left, Ethel
(our actual mother) is nowhere near so
            solicitous of
my brother Leon on *her* lap, and
    Leon knows it too; he looks
as if he suspects she might give him away
            to someone—some *man*—
and above all things Leon loathes men.
    He wants to stay where he is,
secure on Ethel's lap and in Ethel's hands.
        Whereas Jesse, squeezed
    between Ethel and Mother Ida,
        would like nothing better than
for some man to carry him off, any man
            except his father.
Jesse abhors his father, and keeps
        as far away as he can
from the tall tired farmer who will not touch

either daughter with
hands that slaughtered two hogs yesterday,
or was it just this morning?
Those hands of George Gage's look tired too;
in fact, each feature—
his eyes (they're Mother Ida's eyes, only
sunk deeper), those fine black strands
unable to shroud his skull, his leaden lips
drawing the spent flesh
too far down the lantern jaw to smile—
surrenders to the same force
which has already had its incisive way
with Mother Ida;
only his big ears seem unwearied,
crisp with incredulous blood—
Jesse has those same ears, but bigger—bat's ears.
You can't see the mouse
(neither can I) that Jesse fondles
in the cage of his fingers,
but he knows George would genially put it
to an efficient
and unprotestable death with those

strong hands of his, the instant
he discovered his oldest son was keeping
vermin for a pet.
George hates vermin: waste offends.
Between takes, he asks the price
of a bigger photo, one that might include
a kid or two more.
"Unlike you, Gage, I don't enlarge. What I see
is what you get: the print costs the same,
more kids or less. Hold still now."
George subsides. No further questions. His daughters
(pretty Loretta
riding George's right knee, dour Ida
his left) are "with" their father,
of course, while the boys impinge upon Ethel
in appropriate
oedipal array, an alignment
I saluted from the womb:
babies don't need to grow up to recognize
gender in grown-ups—
having one of their own is something
else. That's why they baptized me

Ivory (after the soap: boy *or* girl, I was
                    pure enough to float).
          Of indeterminate sex implies
               "available for either,"
as that other "marvelous boy"—the French one—
                    exulted in his
          immoderate Illumination
               of Dionysus and Co.:
"Graceful son of Pan!"—wonderful, isn't it,
                    the way the phrases
          come unwitting to my weanling lips:
               "How your heart beats in those loins
where the double sex slumbers!" *Le double sexe . . .*
                    But what's the good of
          male and female created He them
               if the great god Pan is dead?
Old mother Ida's out of the running and
                    as far as I know
          I'm not in it, but the rest of us
               certainly show no Eros
to spare, past what's needed for staying alive.
               No, wait: Ethel *smiles,*

ah! the invitation of the flesh:
rubrum, calla, tiger, day.
Consider how they grow, such lilies as these:
they toil to the end
of their days, yet Solomon in all
his glory was not arrayed
like my mother when she smiled into
Disfarmer's eyepiece,
sustaining joy for whatever time
the sacred pose required—
as if a membrane of jubilation had
luminously spread
all across that homely countenance,
endowing the worn but still-
fertile features with an alerted beauty.
And now just look where
our mother's right hand has come to rest,
cradling her son's genitals:
Ecce homo! Ecce ancilla domini!
the sex of the Son
gains an emphasis from the Mother's
guarding hand which shields (yet shows),

in a gesture worthy of Raphael, her boy's
impotent manhood.
In twenty years, Loretta will call
her mother a Jesus-freak,
and Jesse and Ida will desert the farm,
charging George with
"satanic abuses" according
to *recovered memories.*
What have I to do with such charges, such blame?
Mine the sole Eros
unpunished and unpunishable,
for I am like water spilt
upon a table, which with a finger you
may draw or direct
the way you like. What you see here, now,
you cannot get; what you get
will not be seen. *All* families are alike,
the present pursued
by the future, driving it into
the past, pointing at the start
of life to its end as I, all unknowing,
have told it to you.

As we say, out of the mouths of babes . . .
rubrum, calla, tiger, day—
In the beauty of the lilies we all died
in Arkansas, eight
of us here, and the two not yet born:
the present already seen
in the prospect of the past, which will give us
our future at the hands
of Mr. Disfarmer. Funny name . . .
I wonder if I'll meet him
before I grow up and forget . . . Has it all
begun already?

A Thief in the Night,
or Lettres Philosophiques

for Ben Sonnenberg

Nothing is more natural than that
animals should feel and think.
—GEORGE SANTAYANA

i

January third, '02
Happy New Year, Professor Santayana,
or for that matter, Happy New Century!
    (Such a showy way to start,
but I had to begin somewhere: the last thing
anyone learns is what should come first. Perhaps
    not knowing where to begin
is the proper place for beginning . . . Here goes.)
Dear Professor Santayana, it has been
    ever so long since our last

exchange of letters—hardly a *fair* exchange:
yours always so fond and encouraging, mine
        so dismal, so . . . discouraged,
but now I have, for once, news worth *divulging*
(a word "employed" with sinister frequency
        in these offices: I'll try
to live up to the plain sense of the matter).
I really have the sort of news which suggests
        emergence—*my* emergence—
from the cocoon of helpless security
your classes and tutorials propounded
        at Harvard. Not to presume:
no butterfly has emerged—I'm still the same
ever-promising grub I was, and in fact
        I'm now on Grub Street! having
been someone tossing up a coin and waiting
for it to land with a message, except that
        my heads-or-tails are either
a-mind-to-some-purpose or no-mind-at-all—
just a consciousness open at every pore
        to accidents of culture,
what Nietzsche (you told us) liked to dismiss as

"artistic release from the nausea of the absurd."
      So it's not surprising that
my various gesticulations toward "the life
of reason" were really, up to now, nothing
      more than verbatim *dumb show*:
mere mimicry of your smile—a little too
frivolous for philosophy and a lot
      too frivolous for you. Oh,
you *did* let me know (it was the *coup de grâce*)
that my attempt at a *natural perspective*
      resembled nothing so much
as Darwin's last inquiry into "Effects of
Sexual Selection on Syrian Street Dogs."
      A truce to philosophy!
—we both abided by that. I remember
the lull, the feeling of relief literally
      dripping off me . . . What *you* felt
I cannot imagine, after that little
Transformation Scene of ours. Mutual
      was the decision, I'm sure,
that my talents, if they existed at all,
must lie (or is it *lurk*?) in some Other Realm . . .

So for two years now I've tried
being a journalist, and in my office
at the *Times* I've kept tacked up over my desk
    (where I can't help seeing it)
that indispensable axiom of yours:
The material world is a fiction, but any
    other world is a nightmare.
Which discernment made it possible for me
to take seriously my apprenticeship
    at *The New York Times,* and now
it appears that the paper has taken *me*
seriously: I'm to "cover" the lectures
    —seven of them, and in French!—
to be given by the Comte de Montesquiou . . .
No other *Times* reporter, old hand *or* cub,
    knows enough French for the job!
And in light of the Count's lineage, there's not
French enough left over for anyone else
    to know . . . Count Robert *descends*
(by which is meant he manages to get down
to our level) from a nearly endless line
    of Montesquioux so noble

that the Count *condescends* to speak French somewhat
like the rest of us, native to France or not,

  only from higher motives.
Of course you may already know Montesquiou
from your time (or times?) in Paris, when you seem

  to have encountered a great
many of the great (or at least the *gratin*)
during those summers you got out of the Yard.

  If you did meet, most likely
you perceived, among other patrician traits,
the Count's insatiable appetite for cash.

  One newspaper (not the *Times*—
this isn't *Times* style at all) informs the world
that "a well-known impresario has charged

  seventy-five thousand francs
for a set of seven talks by this almost
legendary personage at Sherry's Hotel

  —the inevitable place—
at three p.m. on alternating Thursdays,
tickets 35 dollars for the series,"

  and promises that the Count,
"speaking from the undisputed eminence

of his status in the Faubourg Saint-Germain,
        may reveal the private life
of the whole Parisian *beau monde* from top to
bottom"—though could that world have a bottom?
        I'll endeavor to keep you
au courant de mes recherches approfondies.
Gratefully, as ever, and hopefully, as
        of today,
                your scholar,
                        Jim.

                    ii

        January twentieth
Dear Professor Santayana, already
I've learned more than a mere feature writer
        could presume to know about
Comte Robert de Montesquiou-Fezansac
before the *Cephalonia* has even docked!
        However, I believe less,
now that I've seen the brochure for his lectures
(with a portrait by Whistler on the cover

in rotogravure). I'm told
the original, frame and all, is already
awaiting the Count's arrival in his suite
      at the Westminster Hotel—
apparently he's so smitten with the thing
it has to accompany him everywhere . . .
      Perhaps you saw the painting
when it was "exposed" in Paris, or reproduced
in art journals over here; I'd love to know
      what *you* make of old Whistler
now that he's an Old Master for the very
"art lovers" who once called him an imposter . . .
      Fad or fraud, he's certainly
enlivened the Count's promotional brochure—
a curious document which claims to trace
      the genealogy of
Eustache-Robert de Montesquiou-Fezansac
to Merovingian kings, with a detour
      by way of his (much later)
descent from d'Artagnan himself! At which point
appears, as if by dynastic logistics,
      a choice of the Count's poems

which I challenge even a Harvard professor
to make *anything* of, starting with the title
    (in suitably azure ink)
Les Hortensias Bleues, after a strain of
exotic shrubbery first propagated
    in Paris, though not, it seems,
by the Count. I'm enclosing a bunch of these
hydrangeas (that's our name for them over here)
    for you to rearrange as
you think best while I meet the vessel from which
our horticulturalist will disembark—
    accompanied, according
to the awe-stricken Passenger List, by his
Great Dane and by Don Gabriel de Yturri,
    the young amanuensis
who performs, the Count himself avouches,
"as valiantly in scribal deeds as the Dane
    in defense of my person,"
these very words a sample of Yturri's
virtuosity (or *desperation*?) in
    our so uncouth idiom.
You'd think I could find sufficient copy

in such a *bouquet garni* for some columns
    in the *Times.*

        Wait and see.

             Jim

        iii

   January twenty-eighth
Dear Professor Santayana, Thanks for your
gardener's report on Montesquiou's . . . posies
    (best, I think, to call them that—
when you say "he always sees an exception
before he knows the rule," you leave mere
    criticism in the dust). Thanks too
for your willingness to serve as a sort of
sounding board for my efforts in journalism
    (as you so patiently served
for those sideswipes of mine at philosophy) . . .
When the Count's ship came in—to put it that way—
    it would be hyperbolic
to say there was a *crowd* on the pier, but some
well-dressed onlookers were visibly present

(as I was to learn later,
their presence was due to one of Yturri's
"scribal deeds"); and thereupon we were joined by
Laertes, the steel-gray Dane
sporting an ivory-white leather collar
set with huge garnets (surely they weren't rubies?),
followed by the valiant scribe,
and *then* by their master—monocle, cane and all,
both humans still the worse for *mal-de-mer*, but
not Laertes, who straightway
made for *me* and would not stop licking my hands
(I believe he *had* been seasick after all).
This action was the first sign
of my future *rapport* with the Count's party,
hardly to be counted on (so to speak) by
a mere reporter. It was,
in fact, the dog that prompted what then ensued:
I "must" walk Laertes ("since he's so fond of you")
while the Count gave interviews . . .
After that, Yturri and I in tandem
exercised . . . the hound, and on such outings would
discover how much we were

likely to have in common, the Count being
occupied with the likes of Mrs Astor,
        the indispensable first
to proclaim him a *succès fou*). Then came our
little dinners *à deux* after the lectures,
        the depleted Count having
sought seclusion in his portrait's company:
"*Cette vie publique—on n'est qu'un artichaut,*
        mon cher, lentement effeuillé.
Quant à la condition de mon âme en termes
physiques? Un miroir, un cintre, une porte-plume . . ."
        Which is how M. le Comte
expresses himself once he has surrendered to
the rigors of performance (between clutter
        and complexity he makes
no effort to discriminate—no wonder
people treat his poems so . . . timorously:
        feinting with the damnedest praise . . .)
Here, I think, is where I must put in a word
about Gabriel Yturri, who has served
        this master for two decades.
He's Argentine, and was spirited away

from his country's inveterate "unrest" by
    an English clergyman
working with the Red Cross which charitably
placed him in a Spanish school administered
    by English Dominicans.
And the fact that this superadded language
of his secretary's largely eludes the Count's
    comprehension has fashioned
a bond, an inevitable collusion
between Gabriel Yturri and myself . . .

    And as a result I've learned
that the *causeries* I report so raptly
in the *Times* are a mere *camouflage*—a mask
    for Montesquiou's presence here.
You see, Yturri *talks* to me (in English),
he tells me . . . things, he tells me everything.

    It's a sort of pillow talk—
at least that's how it began, though now he talks
anywhere, everywhere, since No One (*Personne*:
    our code) will be the wiser
for confidences in a language the Count
likes to dismiss as *humiliated French*

or else *German in disguise.*
For Gabriel such converse is a safety valve
—the poor fellow really had to tell *someone*—
and for me revealed the Count's
motive for bringing *that portrait* over here,
as well as the heart of Gabriel's life story
(he can't afford motives and,
to hear him tautologize the terrible
particulars, he hasn't had the kind of
life that has a heart in it) . . .
Back in '85—he was my age then—
he had managed to make his way to Paris,
where he was selling cravats
in an exclusive shop near the Madeleine.
He had (still has) velvet eyes, a peculiar
cooing, guttural accent,
and a longing to genuflect—a genius
for the servitude he accepts to this day.
Montesquiou discovered him
behind an enormous Moreau "Salome"
at the École des Beaux Arts, and thereupon
his fate, as they say, was sealed.

(He is the Count's junior by as many years
as he is my senior now—a coincidence
     which instantly recalled
our own situation at Harvard, and I've tried
to conduct myself with something of the same
     plausible understanding
you showed to a very forward (and of course
very backward) undergraduate back then.
     Professor Santayana,
it may be rude or ridiculous to claim
that you and I shared the same experience
     —even experiences;
yet however diverse they were or became,
I believe we took part in the same structure
     of feeling, the same essence
which will make these maladroit lines of mine
intelligible without your being obliged
     to read too much between them . . .)
Meanwhile, as the novelists say, though you're dead
to rights about the Count's poetic talent,
     or lack of same, I'm convinced,
if only you'd been at Sherry's, you'd agree

that *as a speaker* he has an amazing
    self-promotional aplomb,
chanting like a medieval monk, sobbing
over his own sentimentalities, then
    recovering his self-control
in a voice so theatrical *and* convincing
it easily transmits its possessor's high
    estimation of his words
at the same moment that it insinuates
his disparagement of them. Montesquiou has
    learned the secret of being
a public performer: *he talks to himself*
and lets the audience overhear. Enclosed,
    in wan substantiation,
my *Times* columns of his first two *causeries*
which may suggest what his odd evocations
    of *Vieux Paris* and *Versailles*
were "like," but there's a better story—or worse—
which I'll save for my next installment; by then
    I'll have corroboration
of what is presently just horseplay, hearsay,
and backbiting. Far be it from me to spoil

an authentic scandal by
mere speculation, however apt. Next week,
if Gabriel is still allowed to *talk* to me (all
    other functions having ceased—
the Count *closed down* an intimacy he feared
would somehow betray his manipulations)—
    next week, then, you'll have the tale
as organically as I can tell it—
there's *naturalism* for you, or will be . . .
    Interest piqued?
                Fondly,
                    Jim

        iv

Valentine's Day
Dear Professor Santayana, when I said
there was a shocking story beneath the one
    I've been telling for the *Times*
—a crypt underneath such plausible parquet—
who could have guessed it would turn out to be
    a high-priced penny dreadful?

Not that you, of course, would ever be shocked:
it always seemed to me that true wisdom, as
　　　you practiced or *produced* it,
must mean a certain metamorphosis of
experience, whereby disorder becomes
　　　order of another kind—
another order. George Santayana shocked?
Hardly! Interested, perhaps. Let's hope so . . .
　　　My *ulterior* story
which I'm more or less prepared to tell you now,
although it still shocks *me*, doesn't concern my
　　　amitié amoureuse
with Yturri (if that's what I've been having—
has there been time enough to justify
　　　that helpful French euphemism?),
but a much more unseemly affair. During
these weeks of the awful lectures, and the weeks
　　　between them (for resting up,
as it were, from such exertions, my stabs at
grown-up romance becoming all the while
　　　ever blunter), there occurred
the grand skullduggery I've pieced together

from the Count's exasperated hints and from
     Gabriel's *sotto voce*
exegesis, when he could get out from under
(can this be what I mean?) his *scribal functions* . . .
     It must have all begun . . . No,
I want to speak beyond hypotheticals:
it was in "our" very first class—PHIL. 101—
     that you said, or Plato said
(what difference could it make for me now?):
Beginning is a god who redeems all things
     as long as he lives among men.
Beginning was always a hard place for me,
right from the start of your tutelage. Let's say
     Plato had something; let's say
it all began over a decade ago, when the Count
wrote—in Yturri's English, *ça va sans dire*—
     to Henry James announcing
his imminent arrival in London
and, on the basis of "a word to the wise
     from your friend Mr Sargent,"
requesting in the most obsequious terms
a rendezvous with "*le grand homme*"—with Whistler!

the Count's declared intention
being to visit the Peacock Room and press
upon the painter (there, of course, to receive it)
　　his *panegyrization* . . .
Evidently Montesquiou had no notion
that it was just this intermediary,
　　Henry James *lui-même*,
who, ever so many seasons since, had called
the productions of James McNeill Whistler
　　(and in the *Athenaeum*!)
"uninteresting—they belong to the closet,
not to the world." Exactly what he wrote—.
　　I looked it up—though who knows?
It's quite likely the deracinated old
prestidigitator may have undergone
　　a critical change of heart;
I'd say Mr James's latter-day remarks
on his fellow expatriate were rather . . .
　　benign—they might even be
construed as *approving*, provided one let
the insufferable adverbs have their way . . .
　　In any case (Gabriel

proudly showed me the entire correspondence)
Mr James, putting to good use that wicked
      affability of his,
agreed (won't a novelist agree to anything
if there's a prospect of a story in it?)
      to present to one another
the Bat, Montesquiou's notorious totem,
and the Butterfly, Whistler's fritillary
      reciprocal. . . . Well, in spite
or perhaps just because of such auspices
the occasion (it was at the Reform Club)
      was a sufficient success
to be saluted by subsequent couplets
from the Bat (rhyming *Whistler* with *mystère*),
      whereupon the Butterfly
obliged with yet *another* invitation
to one of his new-fangled Chelsea "brunches,"
      a word Beatrice Whistler
would not speak or hear spoken, but to which
the Count responded rather biblically
      (and here Yturri's English
was not just proper but prophetic): "*I am*

coming among you like a thief in the night
     and at the very moment
when you expect me least." So, with no trouble
at all, the Count's secret design was fulfilled:
     to "commission" a portrait—
oh, nothing so blatant as that word was used,
but it was simple enough for Montesquiou
     to suggest that such a thing:
a—no, *the* portrait—be undertaken straightway
the true purpose, certainly, of the Bat's flight
     to London—why, the thing was as
good as done, the doing was a nobleman's
grace, an artist's privilege, the collusion of
     genius and good manners—
and of course crude contractual terms were skipped
or escaped by the eventual artist
     (who suddenly decided
a studio in Paris would be appropriate
"for the better part of the sittings") *and*
     by the patrician poseur . . .
Isn't that an appropriately lofty cliff
on which to leave you hanging until my next

feuilleton? In any case
I must finish my next feature for the *Times*,
to be followed by the various artistic
  verisimilitudes of
this history. Can you endure the suspense?
I fondly hope so.

                    So, fondly,

                              ever,

                                   Jim

                         v

            February 21
        Dear Professor Santayana,
I realized, just after sending you the last
installment, that I am writing—and *living*!
        (somewhat vicariously)—
two stories at once. Like a Wilkie Collins
heroine—like Marian Halcombe, so puzzled
        about her own part in all
the ongoing villainy . . . One story, for which
I'm responsible (to the *Times*) and culpable

(to myself *and* Gabriel),
is unwinding so "proficiently" that no
comment is required: the terrible lectures
    are given and reported,
and my budding intimacy with Gabriel
is daily betrayed by both parties to it.
    And yet the *other* story
appalled me more, as Gabriel went on with
his description of The Portrait's Progress:
    "a masterwork on canvas . . .
in the frame." Did you know old Whistler painted
all his full-length portraits that way—the figure
    at a depth behind the frame
equal to the distance the artist takes from
his model? Which accounts for the odd title:
    Arrangement in black and gold,
when there's not a trace of gold in the picture,
only the gilding of that enormous frame . . .
    The Count would appear—"*the Bat
will flit to you at sunset*"—and perhaps
in a year the mystery would be . . . revealed!
    Could you believe how many

sittings . . . sessions . . . even *séances* (when the Count
was across the channel, that gray chinchilla cape
    would be held by a model,
though never with quite the requisite absence
of intention, the decorative *brio* . . .).
    Perhaps a hundred poses—
not even a Montesquiou could guess there were
so many. And it was all a great secret—
    the Count would come incognito
to London, using strange aliases and
skulking through alleyways, when he could have
    accompanied a brass band
down Picadilly with no one the wiser . . .
Whistler loved sharing the secret, dissembling
    energetically, though
he had no idea, I'm sure, of the reason
for all this mummery, especially once
    the whole process was resumed
in the rue Monsieur-le-Prince—perhaps it seemed
no more than an eccentricity of caste,
    oddly contradicted by
an expressed longing for the *Chevalier noir*

(that was their pet name for it) to appear
        at the Champ de Mars Salon
the following May—if it was ever done!
As the work "advanced," it became evident
        Whistler himself could not bear
the idea of outsiders in the studio
or of the portrait's ever leaving it—
        an aging artist's qualms, or
perhaps a capricious attachment to his
"late manner"—a fretful mood which nonetheless
        seemed to amuse Montesquiou
who so shrouded himself in mystery no
acquaintance within a three-mile radius
        could have failed to detect him . . .
To Yturri the Count boasted this would be
the last full-length figure from the Master's hand,
        which had hesitated more
than in former days, venturing each new touch
which would then be scraped out, a slow layering
        continuously coddled
by every enigma his brush could deduct
from reality . . . As if the infernal thing

were hidden within the canvas
and Whistler, merely by passing his "wands"
over the surface day after day, summoned
    the magic into matter.
Those were golden hours . . . days . . . weeks . . . months,
as Yturri (always there for whatever
    his master or Laertes,
latest member of that outrageous household,
might require) described them to me. And the Count,
    probably delirious
that his long-laid scheme was likely to become
a reality, ordered Yturri to send
    Beatrice Whistler, in London,
a bracelet of enamel bats (what else?), and then,
learning from her husband of a taste she shared
    with himself, with Mallarmé,
(and with Boldini and Sargent as well) for
Empire furniture, to deliver—to ship!—
    to the Chelsea studio
a great teak boat-bed, festooned fore and aft
with laurel garlands pecked by gilded swans,
    originally given

to the Count's great-grandmother Louise-Charlotte
de Montesquiou by Napoleon himself!
    Professor Santayana,
I make so much of this Aladdin-like
munificence for reasons which I'll explain
    next time. Enough is enough
or even, perhaps, too much?

Yours fondly,

Jim

vi

(March 13)
Dear Professor Santayana, a word
about Montesquiou and magnanimity . . .
    Only money, as they say,
costs him anything—he's wholly generous
with anything he owns, makes, or inherits.
    He cannot *earn* his living—
not a noble activity—and of course
is reduced to terrible expedients
    like giving lectures *abroad*

to obtain the semblance of wealth he *ran through*
ages ago. Yet I've come to understand
    that for my poor Gabriel
he represents the historic past of France
in all its opulence: all the great paintings,
    all the classical dramas,
every last seduction of the intellect—
so that to grant the Count's desires, the Count's *needs*,
    is, for Gabriel, to serve
the creation of beauty and the very
soul of nobility. Yturri delights in
    wearing himself out not just
serving but *enhancing* "the true genius
of Gaul" in Montesquiou's trumpery image.
    (For of course "poor Gabriel"
was in on the scheme of selling to Duveen
for at least a Pretender's ransom—a King's
    being unlikely to raise
much cash—the portrait which appears to have slid
from Whistler's hands into the Count's without
    the latter's ever *paying*
for it, except with his great-grandmother's bed).

There is another view to take of the Count's
    conduct besides Gabriel's
prostrate devotion to his azure blood and
the pretensions of his awful poetry—
    there's the New York Swindle,
an "arrangement," precisely, "in black and gold":
Montesquiou's self-serving fantasy that once
    the usual fusillade
of flattery and vilification had
subsided from the battery of the press,
    the portrait too would vanish
into the Pavillon des Muses in Versailles—
no more to be said, or known, about it—at least,
    no more in England or France—
and thence be disposed of like any other
thing in the possession of a nobleman,
    his to do with as he liked . . .
Imagine, then, the Count's displeasure, having
successfully closed a deal with the Duveens
    the same week the lectures "closed"
(though his performances had been so admired
that *entrée* would be the *mot juste*—to every

mansion of the Four Hundred
from Fifth Avenue all the way to Newport)
—displeasure is too mild a word for it: try
   spasms of indignation,
paroxysms of outrage upon receiving
Whistler's "abusive scrawl" (Gabriel had saved
   every scrap of what the Count
tore to tiny pieces in a fit of noble pique;
here's our patient reconstruction, assembled
   in my office at the *Times*):
"*BRAVO Montesquiou—both your beautiful words*
AND your promised bequest to the Louvre have had
   to yield to Yankee $—
'*Needs Must the Nobly Born will Nobly Do*'
and the portrait you acquired as a Poet,
   for a song, is sold again
as the Jew of the Rue Lafitte, for ten times
that song!—Congratulations, BUCCANEER!"
   Professor Santayana,
once the Count and Gabriel (and Laertes)
leave New York—a frenzy of packing is under way—
   I'll give you more of the facts

which a "family newspaper" must consent
        to spare its readers. The tale
is rather sordid, after all—both tales, but
the reader is not yet born who can resist
        an accurate portrayal
of the expensively seamy side of life.
For now, as newspapers always say: *Later*,
        whatever that means.
                              Love,
                                  Jim

                        vii

            March 23
Dear Professor Santayana, they've all left:
the nobleman and his amanuensis,
        his hound, and the autochrome
copy Montesquiou had ordered once the sale
was set, a full-size print set in a black-and-gold
        frame, very Whistlerian,
though I wonder how the Count can be content
with such a thing in that Pavilion of his . . .

A French art rag, *La Bavarde*,
reported the sale last week, though Whistler seems
to have known the exact amount long before:
one hundred thousand francs,
which probably consoled the Count quite nicely
for the "vile slander" spread by One Knows Whom
in all the Faubourg salons,
though his moods those last days were . . . variable,
and he seldom let Gabriel out of his sight
as you can well imagine.
Yet our *adieux* were mild—until he released
his *mot* he must have prepared (with Gabriel's help)
long before: *"Mon cher ami,*
I don't know how you stand it. The only way
to enjoy life in this cold city of yours
is to burn one's standards and
warm oneself at the blaze. And now I stroll
among the cooling ash of my prejudice . . .
We look forward to seeing
something of you in Paris. Au revoir, Jim."
He left the room, and it was Gabriel's turn,
or my turn with Gabriel.

Professor Santayana, Gabriel *explained*
why he was leaving with Montesquiou, as if
      I had thought he would stay here . . .
In his funny pontificating manner,
he said he had learned—from living with the Count!—
      that true love exists only
between a man and a man, and true sex only
between a man and a woman—and this was why
      he would never leave the Count,
though (as I hastened to tell him) the reverse
situation seemed as likely to apply—
      in fact, *more likely*. No use
arguing with a phony French epigram.
I realize now Montesquiou is a cheat
      through and through, even if
he and Gabriel had decades of "true love"
or "true sex," whatever in hell that may be.
      Professor Santayana,
I just may go—to Paris. Oh, not after
Gabriel. If I'm not for women, I *am*
      against men, and Gabriel
is just a phallus *ex machina*, or was . . .

But my Montesquiou articles have borne fruit,
      if that's the right expression,
and the *Times* has made a Paris assignment
sound very attractive, though I don't suppose
      I'll be presenting myself
at the Pavillon des Muses to thank the Count . . .
For inspiration, as it were. If I go
      —I'm asking you if I should:
your letters during this whole episode
have been so constructive, particularly
      when you said I made you laugh.
Speaking of laughter, I've just read Henry James's
new novel—it's about Paris transforming
      a rather dim young fellow
into a veritable demon of sensibility . . .
Do you think something of the kind could happen
      to me over there? Something
like a final effort at seeing things *tel quel*:
the chick getting rid of its shell . . . My problem
      —I hear you: "*Only one, Jim?*"—
is that what I've had so far aren't perceptions
at all but well-prepared topics that could be

carried around intact. And
wasn't that just my problem (*"another one!"*)
with Philosophy? Dear Professor Santayana,
        maybe I'm like one of those
fanatic creatures we would see on the Common
back in 1900, bearing menacing signs,
        only my sign would be not
menacing but marveling, and it would say
THE BEGINNING IS NEAR! God, I hope so.
        Can you tell I'm trying to
follow in your footsteps? (Unless that sounds
too much like Gabriel.) A thousand thanks for
        your endless patience with your
eternal student, who promises, this time,
to keep in touch wherever he is.

                        My love

                                Jim

A Faun's Afternoon

by Stéphane Mallarmé

translated by Richard Howard

If only these were here forever—nymphs
whose rosy flesh can spur the drowsy air
to dancing.

        Did I love a dream?
                        My doubt,
the residue of all my nights, dissolves
into a maze, merely a budding grove:
proof that what I took for rapture was
a subterfuge of . . . roses.
                  Just suppose
these women had no other reality
than figments of a faun's deluded mind:
illusion seeping like spring-water from
the coy one's cold blue eyes, even as
her sister's sighs were no more than a breeze
fondling my pelt.

And it was all a lie!
No stream arouses from their somnolence
these suffocating fields; it is my flute
whose faltering cascade relieves the grove;
and the only wind, quick to escape these pipes
before the sound spreads in an arid rain,
is—rising serene on the undefiled horizon—
the visible and artificial breath
of inspiration which remounts the sky.

You silent lips of a Sicilian marsh
which like the sun my vanity ransacks,
submissive beneath such radiance, TELL
how as I was harvesting the hollow reeds
my art requires, amid the murky gold
of foliage trailing into far-off pools,
an animal pallor rippled in repose:
and how to the prelude of my untried pipes
that flight of swans—no! of naiads takes wing
or dives . . .

Torpid at tawny noon, the world
smolders: no sign of how they could have fled

the piper's longed-for consummation. Then
must I rouse myself to that first desire of mine,
erect and alone, a lily in the flood
of primal light, ingenuous as *they* . . .

For all this dalliance their lips bestowed
(a kiss, mute witness to their perfidy),
my own breast, innocent of proof, avows
the secret scar of some illustrious tooth—
no more of that! Divine arcana chose
for earthly confidant the reeds I play,
which (taking my cheek's fever for their own)
dream in an endless phrase that I beguile
the beauty of this ringing grove, make false
confusions between it and my credulous song;
creating (as only love, behind closed eyes,
can modulate from ordinary dreams
of belly, back, or unpolluted thighs)
one sonorous, vain, undeviating line.

Malignant Syrinx, instrument of old
evasions, try blooming again, go

back to the pools where you lie in wait for me!
I have my own voice, proudly I shall speak
of goddesses, and by idolatrous
portrayals steal from their shadow veils
and more than veils: thus, once I have sucked
the bright juice out of grapes, I'll banish regret
(which I can at least pretend to cast aside);
laughing and wild to be drunk, I'll hold
the empty cluster up to the sky, inflate
the luminous skins and stare through them till dark.

O nymphs, let us as well inflate our several
MEMORIES: "*Parting the reeds, I would spy
each immortal nape among the waves
and fling a cry of rage to the forest sky;
at which the lovely heads of hair would sink
in shuddering splendor, a cascade of gems!
Later, tangled at my feet and suffering
the languorous travail of being two,
these sleepers lie in each other's random arms.
I fall upon them, seize both at once, and rush
to this staring clump of roses that defy*

immoment shadows, yielding to the sun
their every sweetness: here may our sport
be consummated like the squandered day."
I adore that virginal wrath, O fierce delight
of the sacred naked charge pulling away
from my scalding lips, the lightning-thrust
that probes a secret terror of the flesh:
from the cruel one's feet to the other's
timid heart, abandoned both of them
by innocence drenched in frantic tears
or maybe a moisture less melancholy . . .
"Giddy with conquest of such tears,
my crime is to have overcome these fears,
to have divided the disheveled clump
of kisses that the gods kept so close-mixed:
for no sooner had I smothered a gloating laugh
in the joyous flesh of one (and only held
by one finger, to keep her warm—
while her sister burned—the little naive one
who never blushed), than from my arms,
released as if by death, this thankless prey

broke free, with not a moment's pity for
the sob that held me drunken still."

So what!

Others will take me all the way to joy,
winding the horns on my brow within their curls;
passion knows how, crimson and already ripe,
each pomegranate bursts in a hum of bees;
and our blood, longing for its master, flows
for the whole eternal swarm of our desire.
Now, when this grove is tinged with gold and ash,
a feast is laid among extinguished leaves:
Etna! on your heights where Venus comes,
treading your lava with immortal heels,
the sorry sleep explodes, the flame goes out.

I hold the queen!

For which, sure punishment . . .

No,

but the numb body must submit, the dumb
soul at last succumb to Noon's proud spell:

in sleep all blasphemies are blameless. Sprawled
on the thirsty sand, how greedily I gape
for the sun's inviolable wine.

                              Farewell, nymphs!
Soon I shall see the shadow you became.